A DARKER SHADE OF BLUE

A DARKER SHADE OF BLUE

SEASONS OF LIFE

Saarela Skye

Is It Wet Yet Press

Contents

1

∽

A Darker Shade of Blue : By Saarela Skye

2

~

Dedication

I dedicate this book to all those who feel as though they can't feel happy, sexy, or sad. You can feel any type of way, and any type of color.

3

❧

Chapter 1 : A Colorful Beginning

The Color Red
Fueled by Fire
Remission
Snakes
In This Moment
Dawn of a New Day
Remain in the Shadows
Always With Me
Into The Woods
Beautiful Blue Eyes
Stay Kind
Inner Healing
Perpetually

A Lover of Rain
Rainbow
Colorful Than Ever
The Truth
We Are Everywhere
Medication
To Have Fun
Outplayed
We Are the People
A Better Place
Heaven
I Don't Apologize
For Awhile
Renting Memories
Inner Healing
Angel in The Night

4

Chapter Two: Added Darker Tones

Scandalous
Mental Health
Under This Skin
Doubtful
Leading Me On
Ceiling Fan
Shady
Deadly Weapon
I'll Be Gone
The Monster
So What's Next?
If You Hate Me Now
All of My Glory
Filipino Lollipop
The Next Day
One Night Won't Kill Me

5

~

Chapter 3: The Final Product

The Color Black
Freak
Drowning Me
Please Cut Here
Relapse
High
Praying for my Downfall
Unwell
Saboteur
Living with Anxiety
Obviously, You're the Killer
Life Can be Cruel
Persevere
Disappointed
Take Me Instead

Black Mold
Fade to Grey
Show My Teeth
Enjoy The Day
Phantom
Neon Color
Asylum
Without You Here
Doubtful
Which Mask?
I Can't Keep My Tears From Falling
Dance In Graveyards
Wonderland

6

∽

The Color Red

*T*ell me you love me
*H*ere is my heart
*E*ntangled bodies
*C*an't be torn apart
*O*ur future's bright
*L*ike the blazing sun
*O*r a blinding light

Repairing our past
Repainting this life
Everything is good
Different this time

7

∾

Fueled by Fire

Memories cloud my head,
you are really dead,
regret all I've said,
now I'm the color red.

I'm fueled by fire,
my flames rise higher,
I'm a fighter,
and my aura's brighter.

8

∾

Remission

My emotions have been crazy for reason,
and all the while I've been battling depression.
A lot has changed, especially with my demons,
and now all of my battles are in remission.

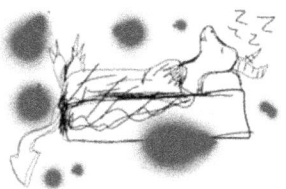

9

~

Snakes

I'm so sick and tired of this world,
there's no one I can't trust anymore.
People act fake, it hurts,
and it's better to be safe and lock the door.

I've learned to trust my gut,
and I've learned to not second guess.
I know that I'm tough
and that I have passed the test.

I will open up to those who are real,
there are just too many snakes in the field.
I stay safe, don't want to be their meal,
and my life won't be theirs to steal.

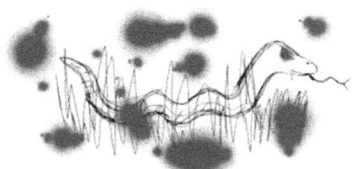

10

In This Moment

I'm laying in a field with you,
the sun is setting,
and there is nothing else I want to do.
The beautiful day is ending,
I'm admiring you,
and I'm glad you're mine.

 The world goes silent,
the moon comes out,
stuck in this moment,
and the night is ours now.

The stars shine down so beautifully
and now all our worries we kiss goodbye.
Tiny spotlights, they're a beautiful sight to see,
a show for us, and no one in sight.
The stars are dancing with us tonight,
no more sadness, not this time,
the stars shine bright for you and me.

11

⌇⌇

Dawn of a New Day

As I wake up,
I already start panicking.
I want it to stop,
I'm worried about everything.

As I stand up,
I feel the ground, it's shaking,
I want it to stop,
and my courage is breaking.

As the days go on,
I feel the warmth of the sun,
I want it to stay,
right next to me and never run.

As I carry On,
a new journey has begun
determination
and strength can't be outdone.

Today, I can finally breathe,
I can just be me.
Today, I can see the light,
the darkness has lost its might.

A new dawn, a new day
all my nightmares fade away.
A new life, a new place.
I am enjoying my new life
today.

12

~

Remain In The Shadows

Everyone is on social media these days,
posting what they're doing,
and retweeting what celebrities say.
That's a complicated lifestyle,
it's hard to stay away,
but I know when to keep a low profile.

Everyone is showing off so much more,
bragging about their diamonds,
and the new color of their front door.
I'm learning to keep my life quiet,
remain in the shadows,
keep everything inside and not share it.

13

Always with Me

Time does heal,
I'm okay for now,
but I'm like steel,
I do break down.

A sunrise helps,
I know you're smiling,

I feel your warmth,
that's you hugging me.

14

∽

Into the Woods

There's a place I go to escape,
it is deep in the woods,
a sacred place.
My soul is rejuvenated,
it is recharged again,
and I start to write.

A place where my art is made.

15

Beautiful Blue Eyes

We both went to high school,
I wore black and had anxiety.
He would dress like a cowboy,
but something about him called to me.

In sophomore year, both in health class,
I'd get nervous when he'd come around.
He had beautiful blue eyes,
and my sexuality I have found.

We both had social media accounts,
I added him and he accepted it.
He'd post things, I'd like them,
and hoped he would get the hint.

Senior year, the final months,
I'd film for class and he'd worked on cars.
He looked so happy, as he always did,
and his smile shined just like the stars.

We both had final projects to do,
I asked if he'd like to be in my film.
He told me that acting isn't his thing,
and it felt like a slap from him.

Now have graduated, living life,
I was committing sins, and he joined the army.
He looked so good in uniform,
and he didn't know what that did to me.

We both are older now and is crazy,
I came out of the closet and he continued to go straight.
He had a few girlfriends, and relationships,
and to like me wasn't fate.

Right now, we are in different worlds,
I'm older, married, and only hope for good.
He's a mechanic, has a wife, a kid,
and now a poem within this book.

16

~

Stay Kind

It's not hard to be a decent human being.
It's not a crime to be a caring person.
It's not a sin to show empathy for others.
It's okay to be a light for the world.

Stay true and stay kind.

17

Inner Healing

Be still my heart, please get some rest,
you are longer put to the test.
Be still my heart, you're finished with your quest,
hush now and sleep within my chest.

Be still my heart, don't overdo yourself,
pain is no longer felt.
Be still my heart, hate is no longer dealt,
now I'll heal and love myself.

18

～

Perpetually

Dancing in our living room,
the heat from the fireplace,
the music resumes,
and this moment we embrace.

Romantic and pure,
it just comes naturally,
forever for sure,
on and on, perpetually.

19

A Lover of Rain

The skies start to darken,
the clouds turn dark gray,
and a storm has awoken,
but that won't scare me away.

The thunder starts roaring,
the lighting is gorgeous as ever.
The rain starts pouring,
I'm in love with this weather.

20

⌒

Rainbow

Red is for the fire inside myself
My flame is so hot I am on fire
Orange is for the warmth I give
I love too hard I want to show it
Yellow is for my bright smile

The world needs to see it more
Green is for how lucky I am
I've got everything I asked for
Blue is my mood some days
I'm human, it's okay not to feel okay
  Purple is my guardian angel
She is watching from heaven

21

∾

Colorful Than Ever

You said I've saved you
and made you change your ways.
You're more alive than ever,
goodbye foggy haze.

I'm what you wished for
and you brought me to life.
I'm more colorful than ever,
the opposite of strife.

22

∽

The Truth

The truth is, I want laughter,
and funny memories,
to remember all of it,
I want to say *I lived my best life.*

The truth is, I want happiness,
give happiness,
and love as well,
I want to say *I changed a person's life.*

23

〰

We Are Everywhere

I am more than my skin color.
I am more than the language I *speak*.
I will always love my culture,
I am the opposite of *weak*.

I am more than what you think.
I am becoming *normal*.
I will always refuse to sink,
I am something not *abnormal*.

I am Asian American.
I am a person of *color.*
You show your ignorance,
and I want peace, I am a *lover.*

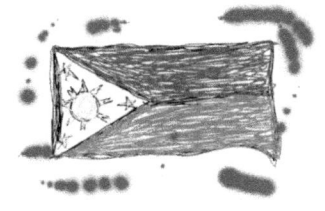

24

～

Medication

Anger isn't a stranger to me,
anxiety isn't a stranger either.
This isn't how I wanted to be,
my mood changes like the weather.

I got the treatment I needed,
200 milligrams do it.
Without it, I would be dead,
and I don't regret it one bit.

25

To Have Fun

I'm my worst enemy,
not that hard to believe?
Too much damage was done to me,
and I'm stuck with constant grief.

I'm my worst critic,
isn't that fantastic?
I beat myself up like John Wick,
mentally ill and mentally sick.

But, you show me so much love
and I'm too far in to just give up.
I have to keep reminding myself,
I have to make time for myself.

It's okay to have fun,
don't feel like I'm on the run,
leave the dark and see the sun,
it's okay to have fun.

26

Outplayed

I'm crawling out of my grave,
my grave that you have made.
You thought you won, and you threw a rave,
but surprise! I'm alive and you've been outplayed.

27

We are the People

Our world has come so far,
people loving, and laughing,
weren't so divided,
and not torn apart.

Now there's no connection,
people crying, hurting,
we're so divided,
I'm sad that this happened.

This is the time we come together.
This is the time we lift one another.
This is the time we fight together.
This is the time we help one another.
His reign, his control won't last forever.

We are the people ,
we are the light ,
and we aren't evil,
we want what's right!

Hear us now,
hear our voice,
sing out loud,
like there's no other choice!
We are the people!

28

A Better Place

I moved to Helena Montana in 2006,
and I wasn't welcomed with open arms.
Was it because my mother was Filipina?
or was it because I was simply an outsider?

I've been bullied and discriminated against,
all because I didn't look like them.
I've been looked at like some sort of plague,
and the locals treated me like I didn't belong.

Those who moved here, those who are a person of color,
may have experienced the same fate.
Believe me, it is getting better,
Helena Montana is a popular spot now.

It is now this present year and I am surprised to still be living here.

more and more people of color are moving to Montana.

The state capital is booming with diversity,

and I couldn't be any happier.

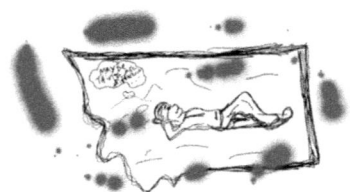

29

Heaven

Heaven does exist,
and it's such a beautiful view.
How do I know this?
Because I see Heaven in you.

30

I Don't Apologize

Sorry, but I don't apologize for being angry.
I don't apologize for the silent treatment.
I don't apologize for my emotions frankly.
And I don't apologize for...

...escaping your mistreatment.

31

Renting Memories

It's crazy how something so great,
can be taken away in an instant.
A shelter full of memories
is now someone else's to have.

It's bittersweet, but a new adventure awaits,
and this adventure consists of many treasures.
No more corrupted humans to hurt us,
and our life will have an abundance of greatness.

32

∽

Angel in the Night

I'm focused on changing my views,
more on the good things, it's true.
Finding a meaning, a long overdue,
angel in the sky, help guide me as you do.

33

∽

Chapter Two: Added Darker Tones

34

～

The Color Blue

I look at my color pallet,
confused, lost, and wondering.
Which color describes right now?
My thoughts are thundering.

Maybe, it's the color red?
angry, loud, and seductive.
How about the color orange?
excited, bright, and productive.

No, it's not the color yellow,
too happy, warm, and optimistic.
Clearly, it's not the color green,
too natural and too simplistic.

I inhale then exhale,
I know this choice is right.
The color that I choose is blue,
calm, true, and just like my night.

35

Addiction

When I first saw you,
I loved the way you looked.
instantly knew,
I'd grow old with you.

When I first kissed you,
I fell so deep,
You made it hard to sleep.
When we first said *I do,*
it was a lie,
and now it is over.

You've married the bottle,
fast, full throttle,
and don't know who've you become.

There's no other outcome.
I thought that you had quit,
still belligerent.
Your addiction got the best of us,
destroying love,
Your addiction is what you want,
you've given up,
and it's what killed us.

36

Can't Keep Up

You pull me in for that sweet kiss,
got me going whoa!
Your tongue circles my tender lips
and chills me to the bone.

I pull away and look into your eyes,
got to tell you now,
I love you don't you realise?
you're shocked somehow.

Here I am, once again,
don't know what to think.
I cannot just pretend,
are you messing with me?

Do you fucking love me,
like I fucking love you?
Are we meant to be,
Are we meant to lose?

Im tired of games,
aren't you tired too?
What you're doing is a shame,
I can't keep up with you.

37

∾

Sexy and Wild

I had a dream of you last night,
it was vivid, and everything I would feel.
I need to relive it, it feels right,
if only this dream was real.

I met you at a late-night barn dance,
a whisky bottle in your hand.
You grabbed my attention with your glance,
and it felt like you had this planned.

You tossed the bottle to your friend,
you made your way to me.
I knew how this was going to end,
I'm the one you wanted to see.

You put your hands on my hips,
we started dancing to the song.
You stared at my cherry lips,
I wanted you all along.

You smirked and grabbed my chin,
your lips made contact with mine.
I got goosebumps on my skin,
you sent chills up my spine.

With your dirty blonde hair and blue eyes,
sexual tension started to grow.

I wanted you between my thighs,
you knew, then you said *c'mon let's go.*

You led me to an empty place,
there was hay scattered everywhere.
You laid me down with such grace,
we undressed, and our bodies bare.

You kissed me as if I mattered,
and you made your way inside.
Your rhythm grows much faster,
Ecstasy I could not hide.

Both of us were sweating,
I heard your moans, you heard mine.
I was close you had me begging,

you made me laugh, and made me whine.

You locked lips with me once more,
your final thrusts made me release.
You pulled out and lay on the floor,
after our climax, the vibrations cease.

I wanted you between my thighs,
you knew, then you said *c'mon let's go.*

You led me to an empty place,
there was hay scattered everywhere.
You laid me down with such grace,
we undressed, and our bodies bare.

You kissed me as if I mattered,
and you made your way inside.
Your rhythm grows much faster,
Ecstasy I could not hide.

Both of us were sweating,
I heard your moans, you heard mine.
I was close you had me begging,
you made me laugh, and made me whine.

You locked lips with me once more,
your final thrusts made me release.
You pulled out and lay on the floor,
after our climax, the vibrations cease.

We both were breathing heavily,
you turned to me and smiled.
We dressed and parted ways pleasantly
and that was my dream, sexy and wild.

38

~

Manipulation

So you can take and take and take
all of my hope you dirty little snake.
So you can lie and lie and lie,
you really fucked up this time.

Go ahead and paint me out as the bad guy,
they won't hear my explanation,
All of their love you buy,
you're the master of manipulation.

39

Superhero

Here is what I've learned:
When you can't depend on others,
just depend on only *yourself*.
 I've studied their ways,
they only care when it's beneficial,
in short, be your own *superhero*.

40

I Don't Care

I don't care about your beer,
your car,
your career,
or if you're a star.

I don't care about the money,
the bills,
if I'm lucky,
or the thrills.

I.
Don't.
Care.

41

～

The Perfect Fit

You know who I am,
I know who you are,
you're a bad idea,
and I bear painful scars.

I avoided you,
you would never quit,
I opened up my heart,
and you're the perfect fit.

42

～

Swearing

I've been a naughty little kitten,
rubbing on you in the kitchen.
You're drinking, naked, and cooking,
my restraint is breaking.

I've been a naughty little turkey,
foraging for your kiss, dirty.
You're melting, aroused, sweating,
I'm on my knees and you're swearing.

43

~

Only an Illusion

I thought I've found the one,
though I've found true love,
you were only an illusion.

...only an illusion

I thought we were doing great,
and thought that this was fate,
but it was only an illusion.

...only an illusion

44

~

A Darker Shade of Blue

You told me we'd paint the world,
we would find all the pearls,
but that was all a lie,
now I sit alone and cry.

I told you my favorite color,
I thought that we knew each other,
but now all thanks to you,
I'm a darker shade of blue.

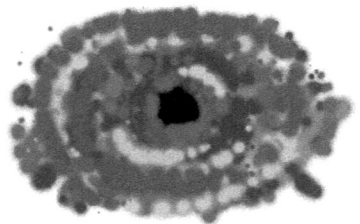

45

～

Scandalous

Working so much, I forgot how to love,
how to enjoy things, and smile.
That's when you walked in, I felt something,
something that had been missing for a while.

I felt new, excited, and rebellious.
I've been stuck on cotton candy clouds,
I felt your darkness, it pulled me down,
and I fell hard and hit the ground.

Something possessed me, I walked over to you,
something inside of you knew what was next.
You grabbed my hand, I held my breath,
and we both were naked and made love on your desk.

46

∾

Mental Health

They claim to understand mental health issues,
but I mean, do they really though?
When I don't feel like hanging out or being social,
they get offended and say *whoa!*

Now I'm the bad guy with an attitude,
I guess they forgot, it happens.
That's when I lose patience, get overwhelmed,
panic and everything blackens.

47

~

Under This Skin

On the surface, I may look tough,
but sometimes I don't give enough.
On the surface, I pretend so well,
acting fine, but I'm going through hell.
On the surface, I seem just fine,
but internally I've lost my shine.

Look into my eyes,
you can see my pain,
can you not see it?
Am I going insane?

Under this skin, I'm hurting,
I've given up,
and I'm completely shattered.
Under this skin, I'm screaming,
filled with regret,
and wishing my existence mattered.

48

∾

Leading Me On

You're so good at leading me on,
you have me thinking there's something more.
Inside, I want all of these feelings gone,
but to you, I'll always be your whore.

49

Ceiling Fan

Everybody's busy and it's raining outside,
Fuck I'm so lonely, hate feeling so confined.

Everybody's sleeping and it's only me,
Fuck I feel like crying, can someone set me free?

I'm learning how to love myself again,
especially after all the shit you put me through.

You've messed me up, I can't pretend,
hurting me is what you love to do.

My thoughts start racing, intrusive thoughts,
These pills are helping, and the pain is lost.

I fall into the couch, songs escape my mouth,
here's a different plan, I'm watching the ceiling fan.

50

~~

Shady

He told me to keep us on the low low,
he loves it when I'm on my knees, below.
His family doesn't know about our hookups,
if they did, they would all be shaken up.

He disappeared for an entire month,
but now he's back and on the hunt.
His life has been rather shaky,
and he's been nothing but shady.

51

Deadly Weapon

Ripping my heart out
and breaking my soul,
there's pain all throughout,
and that was your goal.

Destroying my heart,
you're a deadly weapon.
Planned this from the start,
you'll never reach heaven.

52

I'll Be Gone

I used to love this place,
but now it's pure hell.
I'd rather hide my face
because things aren't going well.

I'm not your personal slave
and I'm not your pawn.
It's best that you all behave,
or I swear I'll be gone.

53

~

The Monster

Meeting you for the first time,
you looked at me in question,
you saw me as a crime,
and there was a little bit of tension.

Eventually, you gave me a home,
and I started to feel better about life.
Finally, I didn't feel so alone,
and that ended quickly, I lost my light.

Corrupted and a lair,
you only want money.
You set me up for failure,
you're so evil it isn't funny.

Revealing the monster you are,
I see your dark and sinister ways.
Seeing that you lack a heart,
karma will follow you to the end of the day.

54

~

So What's Next?

Tie my arms,
tape my mouth,
cause me harm,
you're allowed.

Lick my cheek,
kiss my thigh,
I'm so weak,
I'm so high.

Spank my ass,
bite my neck,
love your sass,
so what's next?

55

If You Hate Me Now

If you hate me now,
you're about to hate me even more.
My face will be everywhere,
my name will be talked about, galore.

If you had shown some love,
you would be sitting right next to me.
Instead, you now sit alone,
and that's where you want it to be.

56

All of My Glory

I'm selling my soul one day at a time,
making a profit off of my stories.
I must say, I'm good at writing rhymes,
some will hate me and all of my glory.

57

∾

Filipino Lollipop

You're licking me up and down,
I'm your Filipino lollipop.
You kiss all of my sweet spots,
and I beg you to never stop.

You're sucking on my nipples,
and I intensify my grasp.
You love to bite my muscles
so I let out a whine and gasp.

You make me feel like royalty,
I've never felt like this before.
I'm living out my fantasy
and I want you more and more.

58

∼

The Next Day

Waking up to smoke and empty bottles,
I lay here naked and alone.
Not something out of a romance novel,
another name goes unknown.

Wondering if this is all still worth it,
feelings do in fact get in the way.
Some days are easier than others,
and there are no regrets the next day.

59

∽

One Night Won't Kill Me

With all of the nightmares
and all of the voices,
my demons are everywhere.
With all of the pressure,
all of the nudgings,
my demons have made it clear.

With all of the chaos,
all of the trauma,
My demons are never lost.
With all the sadness,
all of the torment,

My demons know what I want.
Just one more night,

one more night,
I will be fine.
This is the last time,
just one more night,
this will be the last time.

One night won't kill me,
Everything will be fine,
After this, I'll be alright,
one night won't kill me.

60

Chapter Three: The Final Product

61

～

The Color Black

I try to let go of all of the bad,
trying to look forward and not back.
No matter how many colors I add,
my painting of life is still black.

62

∾

Freak

The curtains open and I'm standing here.
I'm showing my colors, it's everywhere.
A venue full of people, a sold-out show,
out their mouths, profanities they throw.

Another night, another show,
and the feeling of anxiousness won't go.
Everything replays once more
and I'm giving them an encore.

I'm feeling like I'm a part of a circus
and I'm upfront and center stage.
People begin laughing, I can't focus
and I'm flooded with rage.

I'm a freak, I'm a freak
and that's what *I'll ever be.*
I'm a freak, I'm a freak
and that's what *they think of me.*

63

∾

Drowning Me

These past few years were a wild one.
I now know the true colors of people,
and it showed me that life is fragile,
and everything always has a cost.

There is now a dark cloud above my head
and my emotions are like a rainstorm.
Everywhere I look there's water,
it's rising and I'm unable to move.

From a rainstorm to now an ocean
and I'm losing, forced to tread water.
I get pulled under, I'm terrified,
and the ocean I've created is drowning me.

64

∽

Please Cut Here

It's 3 am,
insane goddamn.
Drenched in sweat,
can't forget.

Silent, alone,
a quiet phone.
Terror, fear,
please cut here.

65

∽

Relapse

Cognition isn't right,
dimming is my light,
here I am with fright,
I am losing my fight.

Turning to my cure,
something just so pure,
this will help for sure,
can't take the detour.

This will fill the gaps,
there's no time for naps,
and this might all collapse,
once more I relapse.

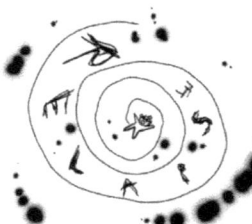

66

~

High

high
Honestly, I love to stay
and don't want to stay

down.

Honestly, I would rather die,
than stay sober forever.

67

∾

Praying for my Downfall

Affirmations and making a difference,
my stories are meant to be relatable.
There are those who wish me bad,
and secretly

*praying
for
my
downfall.*

68

Unwell

Lately, I've been waking up in a sweat,
having dreams of torment and regret.
I don't know what is wrong with me
and I hope I can go back to who I used to be.

Lately, I've been screaming myself awake,
been having nightmares where I do not wake.
I don't know why this keeps on happening,
someone please help me, give me anything.

I'm so ill, sick, I'm puking my guts out,
I'm spiraling and falling to the ground.
A cure is something I need to find,
so I can leave this illness behind.

I've been weak, I've been extremely tired
and I just want to get much higher.
I haven't been me, you can tell
and I'm a sickness, I'm so unwell.

69

∾

Saboteur

Breaking out of their control,
I'm no longer force-fed their constant lying.
All of the houses are painted the same,
an illusion that I'm not buying.

Grabbing my paintbrush, and black paint,
I'm painting large black Xs on all the doors.
Time to expose the truth, I won't back down,
they try to stop me and call me a saboteur.

70

〜

Living with Anxiety

Living with anxiety is like driving at night,
while it's super foggy and unable to see the road.
Living with anxiety is like trying to figure out
which wire to cut as a bomb is about to explode.

71

~

Obviously, You're the Killer

You're acting very suspicious right now,
your invitation I should have disallowed.
We're sitting in this mammoth room,
will this place be my eternal tomb?

The lights go dark,
this whole thing is familiar.
an end to our story arc,
and obviously you're the killer.

72

~

Life Can Be Cruel

I am so heartbroken,
to the point where I cannot breathe.
I am so torn apart,
ripped to thin little shreds believe me.

I am so choked up,
to the point where I cannot talk.
I am so beaten down,
my bones are broken and I cannot walk.

I am so distraught,
to the point where I feel like dying.
I am so depressed,
today I do not feel like living.

Im so unsure,
to the point where I feel like dying.
I am so damaged,
life can be cruel and I know I'm
right.

I am so drained,
to the point where I've given up.
I am lost,
where do I go? I've had enough.

How do I adapt?
How do I carry on with anything?
You were my rock,
You were my rock,

73

Persevere

My blood is on the snow,
wounds caused by you,
I really hope you know
that I persevere through and through.

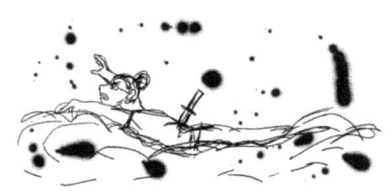

74

Disappointed

Are any of them my friends?
Hard to tell in a world that pretends.
I thought we all agreed to be true,
but now I am disappointed with all of you.

75

~

Take Me Instead

Here is one thing I know for sure
and that is she doesn't deserve this.
She is an angel, a soul so pure,
is there any way to get rid of this sickness?

There is one thing I know I want
and that is for you to heal her now.
Without her you know I'll be lost,
I'm begging, I surrender and bow.

Please, please don't take her,
she has so much more to live for.
Please, please don't erase her,
the world still needs her more.

Just take me instead,
and I'll gladly take her place,
just take me instead,
I've been a huge disgrace.

Don't give her those wings,
 please don't open the gate.
Those wings she doesn't need,
just take me and change her fate.

76

✁

Fade to Gray

The sun rises and the light hits my face,
it's warm and inviting, and my worries are erased.
Something happens, the light fades away,
and fear and depression wrap me in its embrace.

Pain surpasses, it has gone away,
and I rise from the ashes, I will be fine today.
Once again it happens, my colors fade to gray
and my strength simply dissipates.

77

*

Black Mold

My mind hasn't been mine lately
and I want to take back control.
Suffering so greatly,
reclaim my soul you stole.

My thoughts have been chaotic
and my color isn't bold.
Acting so psychotic,
I'm covered in black mold.

78

Show my Teeth

Chained and sent down to hell,
underground, underneath,
small cuts begin to swell
and it's time I show my teeth.

79

~

Enjoy the Day

In my room filled with colorful smoke,
I lie in bed and stare at my ceiling.
Regretting the truth that I spoke,
I know I was too forward and revealing.

In my head, it doesn't seem too loud,
I act as though everything's okay.
Sadness has me bound,
I'm crippled trying to enjoy the day.

80

∼

Phantom

Watching shadows on my wall
and I'm thinking about you.
Without you here, my skin crawls,
and I know what I must do.

Moving my hand down my side,
I imagine you are here.
You grab onto it so tight
and talk dirty in my ear.

Playing scenes inside my head,
and it's you on top of me.
I'm sweating, panting in this bed,
as I set your phantom free.

81

∽

Neon Color

Being confident is one thing
and being cocky is another.
You can be so overbearing
like a neon color.

82

∽

Asylum

Therapy won't help me,
I'm just a lost cause.
killed who I used to be
and I can't return to who I was.

I've lost my heart,
I'm called evil by some,
messed up from the start,
so take me to the asylum.

83

Without You Here

Snow is on the ground,
cold is all around,
and it's only me now.
Leaves begin to fly
and disappear from sight,
just like your light.

The pain comes and goes,
and sometimes it doesn't show
unless I'm alone.
Wish I could change fate,
nothing has been the same,
ever since you went away.

I go through all the seasons,
and all of the holidays,
thinking of a million reasons
why you should have stayed.
I know you want me to go on,
and live without fear,
but that's hard to do without you here.

84

Doubtful

I used to be fearless,
but now I'm soulless,
my future is dim
and it's all thanks to him.

All thanks to him,
my future is dim,
I used to be youthful,
but now I'm old and doubtful.

85

Which Mask?

I go through my closest
and try to pick one that fits the vibe.
There's no way around this,
fool everyone, believe I'm alright.

This mask is too happy,
this mask is too sad,
this mask is too crazy
and this mask is too mad.

Which mask should I wear today?
help to cover my pain,
make me look sane,
something that makes me look okay.

These masks are all built to last,
show smiles and laughs,
and hide the scars I have,
I cherish all of these beautiful masks.

86

∽

I Can't Keep My Tears From Falling

Every day I wish this was just a nightmare
and maybe one day I will wake up from it.
Being alive, and breathing doesn't seem fair,
I want to give up and quit.

I remember you talking about karaoke
and singing with your friends.
You talked about getting healthy,
but your story had a different end.

I can't keep my tears from falling,
I feel like I am suffocating,
this is killing me,
a long future was for you to see.

87

~

Dance in Graveyards

Usually, most people avoid haunted places,
eerie, and scary, and don't know what to expect.
I'm not like most people, I explore abandoned places
and dance in graveyards with nothing but respect.

88

Wonderland

I followed you into the storm,
and my trust began to form,
you promised we'd be okay,
but this loop just replays.

As I close my eyes,
the pain subsides,
I start to fall
and I don't care at all.

I've landed in Wonderland,
in a dream, holding roses in my hand.
I found joy in this strange land,
I found my place here in Wonderland.